Grow Into Success

By: Lyndell Johnson

Copyright

GROW INTO SUCCESS. Copyright © 2018 by Lyndell Johnson.

Published by B.O.Y. Publications, Inc.
P.O. Box 1012
Lowell, NC 28098

Printed in the United States of America

ISBN: 978-0692052686

DEDICATION

This book is dedicated to my wonderful wife, Otescia.
Thanks for believing in me. I love you always and forever.

Acknowledgements

I would first like to thank my wife, Otescia, for being such an inspiration for writing this book. Your work ethic and accomplishments have motivated me to grow and pursue my own dreams, and I can't thank you enough for that.

I would also like to thank our friend and editor, Charita, for her tireless efforts in making sure our books were professionally edited. Your friendship means the world to us.

Many thanks to all my family and friends for supporting me in my endeavors over the years, and helping me to believe that I could do anything. To my children, Omari, Eric, Abriah, Janae, Adonis, and Elijah, you guys are awesome, and I thank you all for your support and confidence.

TABLE OF CONTENTS

INTRODUCTION

In a world full of uncertainties, there is one thing I know to be certain. If you want to be successful in this life, you must grow. When I say grow, I don't mean from a physical standpoint, I mean habitually. Successful people aren't normally born that way. They learn certain success habits and principles that ultimately push them into their life's purpose.

You can adopt those same habits and principles to boost your life to the next level. You are capable of so much more than you think, and I want to help you achieve your highest aspirations. Success doesn't only belong to a special group of privileged people, it's for you too! Greatness has lived inside of you since you took your first breath, you just have to give birth to it.

Giving birth to greatness may be an uncomfortable process. It may come with labor pains and complications along the way, but once the process is complete, you will love the finished product. You will be happy that you chose to grow beyond your comfort zone, and into the realm of limitless success. You are destined to dominate the game of life, and this is your playbook. Use what you read here as a guide to making yourself legendary.

WHAT THIS BOOK CONTAINS

In this book, I have laid out ten necessary principles to get you where you want to be in life. Your goal may be one that is considered easy to reach, or one of those coveted but seldom realized dreams. Whether you want to be a bus driver or a movie star, you will need these tools to navigate your road to success.

Anyone that has ever achieved anything great in life has not done so by accident. It was no mystical event that granted them their heart's desire. They worked hard for it! They created a plan, figured out the tools they needed to make it happen, then got it done. They set out on a journey to find life's treasures, and never stopped until they found what they were looking for. This is the only way to ensure the success you deserve, to keep pursuing your destiny until you achieve it.

In this book, I have included personal stories of triumph, as well as stories of others who have climbed life's mountain and planted a flag, staking their claim to what rightfully belongs to them…FREEDOM! Freedom to do work that they love, freedom to leave a legacy to their families, freedom to affect change in the lives of others, and freedom to obtain greater happiness than they have ever known.

It is my sincerest hope that you will enjoy this book. Every page was written to inspire you. There is a hidden potential buried deep within each of us. I want to teach you, through this book, how to access that potential and use it to grow into success!

Chapter 1
COMMIT TO THE PROCESS

"Commitment is what transforms a promise into reality"
- ABRAHAM LINCOLN

Are you committed to making your dreams come true? Not just committed to saying what sounds good, but committed to actually ***MAKING*** your dreams a reality? Many people lounge around hoping and wishing that lifelong dreams will magically materialize before their eyes. We all know people who fit into this category. They corner you at gatherings to discuss their dreams, but never put forth the required effort to make things happen.

As a society, we see celebrities living lives that we only fantasize about. Big houses, fancy cars, and lots of money seem to be out of reach for the average working-class citizen. We think we can never live the good life, but the truth is, we can live however we decide to live. If we choose to be miserable, hating to wake up every morning, then that will be our fate, a miserable life that drains us of positive energy. However, if you decide to live better and not give in to your current circumstances, you can break free of that mold and carve your life into a work of art that you can be proud to say you created.

It's up to you to commit to the process. You must commit to taking the first steps on your journey into purpose. We often want to get to the end result without taking the steps, but until you take the first steps, there can be no journey. You will never build the necessary momentum that could propel you into what you perceive as impossible if you aren't actually moving in the direction of that which you seek.

When I first committed to writing this book, I was petrified. My mind was filled with thoughts of self-doubt. I wondered to myself, can I really do this? Who am I to give other people advice on how to improve their lives? I soon realized that the value of my own life experiences qualified me to write this book. I've been on a journey towards the completion of this book since the moment I decided to put the principles I'm sharing with you into practice in my own life. Putting the principles in practice was my first step. What will be your first step?

THE RESOLVE ON THE INSIDE

There must be a resolve within your heart that pushes you into commitment. I must warn you though. This is no ordinary commitment. This is a commitment that shifts your very being from a bystander that watches life pass you by, to a benefactor of life's infinite rewards. You have so much greatness on the inside of you in the form of ideas that if you were to dig them from within, you could become a millionaire many times over. But it all starts with a simple commitment.

Commitment can take you from a humble beginning to an epic ending. If you seek more recognition, more love, more money, more of whatever you wish for, it's all available to you if you commit to going after it. Decide that you will not be denied, because if someone else can obtain great things out of life, so can you! You have the power to fashion your future. You are a creator with the ability to draw your own blueprint for success. It all depends on your mindset and knowing that you are capable of being a trailblazer that forges your own path to abundance.

COMMIT TO WEATHERING THE STORM

Storms will come, but they are not meant to stay. They are meant to pass by and make you stronger. Just as weather storms come to bring balance to nature, the storms in your life come with purpose. They are rough for a moment, but calm skies are always on the other side. There will come times when you want to give up, but commitment can and will pull you through.

When discouraging thoughts flood your mind, allow that commitment to be the vessel that carries you through the murky waters of doubt. Let your commitment to creating a magical life be the fuel that helps drive you into your promise land. Master the habit of welcoming storms, because many will come your way. You just have to be committed to conquering them.

My wife and I have had our fair share of storms in our lives. Our biggest storm came when I got out of the Army back in September 2011. My wife was working as an office manager for a business in our area. Things were going great. She would routinely receive nice bonuses for her stellar performance on the job, and our financial situation seemed secure. Fast forward to 2013, the company my wife worked for was acquired by another company. Her boss, who was also the seller of the company, assured her that she would be able to keep her job. She even received a raise when the new company took over, which made the takeover seem like a blessing in disguise.

Soon after, the storm winds began to blow. Out of the blue, my wife received a phone call from the Vice President of the company. No notice, not even an in-person conversation, just a phone call to say her office was being shut down immediately. Her heart hit the floor. All the hard work she had put in for the company meant nothing to her bosses as they snatched away our livelihood with a single phone call. We were crushed. My income had already taken a hit, so we were barreling towards financial disaster.

A few weeks later, I got a job working in a transportation dispatch call center. This seemed to be the answer to our prayers. I was making more money than I ever made on a civilian job. Little did we know this blessing would only last about two months, and our mortgage payment would be due again soon. What were we going to do? As I'm sure every parent knows, the most difficult moment in a parent's life is the moment they have to wonder if they'll be able to continue providing a home for their child(ren). We were no exception. Our children were accustomed to a lifestyle we worked hard to create for them. The storm was threatening to take that lifestyle away. We are a family of eight. If we lost our home to foreclosure, where would we go? Our family is too large to live with relatives while we get back on our feet, and quite frankly, my wife and I could never see ourselves burdening anyone in that manner.

We ended up renting our house to a friend, and relocating to California. While there, my wife and I both found jobs and started putting our finances back in order. It took a while, but we were able to get back on track before moving back to North Carolina after the storm had passed. During this storm, my wife and I faced the worst financial crisis of our marriage, but we came out stronger on the other side. We even became closer to each other throughout these hard times. Because of our commitment to persevere during our darkest hours, we were strong enough to triumph over life's tragedies.

WHY IS THE ANSWER

You may be asking yourself what you need to do to make it through your storm. What must you do to move closer to the life you seek? The answer is also a question, that when answered, will catapult you into an elevated state of motivation. This question is the starting point for your journey. Just ask yourself why.

❖ Why do I want to be successful?

❖ Why should I commit to this process?

❖ Why should I invest in my own personal development?

❖ Why should I commit to breaking out of my comfort zone?

People have a wide variety of answers to these questions, some of which are as follows:

❖ I want to travel the world.

❖ I want to be able to retire early.

❖ I want to become the best version of myself.

❖ I want to leave an inheritance for my children.

These whys can be great inspirations for achievement. As human beings, we are all wired to be motivated by our whys. But a lack of why can also leave one unmotivated. I think most parents may have seen this principle in action when asking their child why they did something they were asked not to do.

I was once faced with this situation when I asked one of my teenage sons to stop doing something. When he did it again, I asked him again to stop doing it and explained why I wanted him to stop doing it. When I asked him why he didn't just listen to me the first time I asked him to stop, his response was, "You didn't tell me why I needed to stop." Even though he is a teenager, he has that same innate drive we all possess. He needed a why to motivate him to do what he was being told to do. Your why is what will motivate you to continue your journey even when storms make you want to abort the process.

A PORTRAIT OF COMMITMENT

Retired boxer, Floyd Mayweather Jr., is the richest boxer of all time. As a teenager, he was an Olympic boxer, who was also the National Golden Gloves champion in 1993, 1994, and 1996.

Mayweather was born on February 24, 1977 in Grand Rapids, Michigan. Born into a long-line of boxers within his family, Floyd has been trained to fight since he was a young child. Although he

19

grew up poor, while living under difficult circumstances that would have discouraged most, Floyd knew that he was destined for huge success in the world of boxing.

When he was nineteen, Mayweather decided to turn pro. Within his career, he made a commitment to be the best pound for pound boxer in the world. This was a very lofty goal, but Floyd saw no limits for himself. He committed to training like no other and took the necessary steps to get to the top of his field. He could frequently be seen partaking in grueling training sessions that were open to the public. Although he is considered the greatest boxer of his time, his idols are not other boxers. Floyd's idols are businessmen like Bill Gates and Warren Buffet.

The boxer/businessman's commitment to excellence in and out of the ring benefited him tremendously, because at the time of the writing of this book, he has retired with an undefeated record of 50-0 and a net worth of around $400 million. He also founded his promotion company, Mayweather Promotions, in 2007 which promotes sporting, live music, and theatrical events, as well as television and movie productions.

Mayweather's story is one of the many examples that prove anything is possible. Armed with a bulletproof commitment to excel and achieve greatness, you can do and be whatever you want in life!

Grow Into Success

You can manipulate your universe into the best thing since sliced bread, if you would only make an ironclad commitment.

<u>RECAP OF COMMITMENT</u>

1. Come to a resolve of commitment within yourself.

2. Commit to weathering the storms of life.

3. Accept that your why is the answer.

4. Follow Floyd Mayweather's example of commitment.

5. **FULLY COMMIT TO THE PROCESS.**

Chapter 2
PINPOINT YOUR PURPOSE

"Success demands singleness of purpose"
-VINCE LOMBARDI

Roughly seven billion people inhabit this planet, and every man, woman, and child has a certain purpose that they are destined to fulfill. Many go through their entire lives never learning what their purpose is. They fail to figure out what they are meant to contribute to this world they live in.

The problem with never learning your purpose is that life is hard. It can deal you some serious blows that seem impossible to bounce back from. Some experience death in their families that end up crushing their spirits, some lose expensive material possessions, while others suffer failed businesses and careers, which makes them believe their life is over. Not understanding your purpose can leave you thinking that the only reason you were born was to endure heartache and grief, which may tempt you to throw in the towel.

If you plan to find happiness in the future, you must pinpoint what your purpose is. You must seek out what you were born to do and chase it with every fiber of your being. Capture that elusive enigma that has puzzled you your entire life and make it bend to your will.

THE SUPERHERO COMPARISON

When I was a child, I wanted to be just like Superman. I thought he had a cool costume, he was strong and fast, plus he could fly. Who wouldn't want to be like Superman? What I didn't know as a child was that in addition to all the cool superpowers he had, Superman also had a purpose. He had something that he knew was his life's mission, and he was willing to die for it. Just like all other superheroes, Superman's purpose in life was to do good for the world around him. He encountered adversities while enhancing and saving the lives of others using the gifts that he was born with.

We as humans are comparable to superheroes. Our core purpose as a species is to contribute to the world by doing good using our gifts and talents. What is your gift? Whether you are a doctor that is gifted in healing the sick and wounded, or a business owner that alleviates the pain points in a customer's life, you can be a superhero. You can be the one who swoops in and saves the day when the world seems to be falling apart. Being a superhero who is grounded in purpose comes with both challenges and rewards. Here are some of them.

1. Supervillains Will Come Against You

Supervillains are those that work to hinder progress towards the superhero's purpose. You will encounter these villains in the form of haters. They will despise the good that you try to do in the world, and will exhaust all their efforts and resources to stop you from making a difference.

In the cartoons and comic books, superheroes fight supervillains in order to fulfill their purpose. Superman fought multiple supervillains to keep Metropolis safe, and Batman fought The Joker, The Penguin, Bane, and many others to keep Gotham City safe. Although heroes fought in the comics, you as a superhero don't have to. When your supervillains/haters strive to thwart your efforts to move in your purpose, you should simply ignore them and keep pushing forward.

Unlike the comics and cartoons, fighting against your supervillains/haters gives them strength. It motivates them to see you upset, discouraged, and wasting your energy on them. The best offense against haters is a closed mouth and forward movement. Keep advancing towards what you are supposed to do, and silence your haters with results that are undisputed.

2. You Have Vulnerabilities

All superheroes have something that makes them vulnerable. These things include: Kryptonite for Superman, anything yellow for Green Lantern, a weak heart that requires energizing for Iron Man, and being human for Batman. Although we may not share many of these vulnerabilities, we all have something that makes us weak. A flaw that we must overcome to be at our best.

Some of our vulnerabilities are: Criticism, self-doubt, harmful habits, selfishness, anger issues, and overwhelm from daily pressures. These are all personal issues that can veer us away from our purpose if we let them. When we are self-aware of what holds us back from what we are called to do, we empower ourselves to do the things that can eliminate these obstacles. I encourage you to do an honest inventory of what weakens your ability to serve your purpose and work on mitigating these issues, so that you can shine bright and be the superhero that you are supposed to be.

3. You Are Strong

Some superheroes have extraordinary physical strength that is beyond measure, but you have extraordinary strength inside of you that makes you a phenomenon. You can achieve anything that you desire bad enough. If you want to multiply your income by ten it can be done with a solid plan of action. Your real power stems from your mind. You are a juggernaut with the mental capacity to literally redirect your life's path, but you must utilize your powers to do so. You must understand that you are a force to be reckoned with, and that no life circumstance or unfortunate situation can keep you tied in turmoil.

There is no stronger power than the human spirit. We can rise when we get knocked down, and create a way where no way seems to exist. Exercise your cognitive muscles and commit to consistent growth. Reading books and blogs, and brainstorming fresh ideas for your future will make your brain stronger. Decide that you will manifest the miracles that you want to see. You are in control of this ride called life, and you must be willing to take the wheel and steer yourself in the right direction. And although you don't have Superman's strength, you do have a strong mind that yields unparalleled power to fulfill your life's purpose.

DESTINY IN DISGUISE

When I was a child, my mother would frequently ask what I wanted to be when I grew up. My answer was always the same. I wanted to be a doctor. I liked the white coat and stethoscope, and doctors just seemed to be nice people. I was drawn to the profession throughout my childhood, and thought that my purpose was to help heal people and save lives through means of medicine.

Lyndell Johnson

Once I entered my teenage years, my perspective changed. I no longer wanted to be a doctor, because I wasn't a fan of seeing blood and dealing with patients. I wanted to be a rapper. I immersed myself in the hip hop culture and thought this craft might be what I was made for. It was the only thing I thought I was good at. The truth was that I saw music as an opportunity to become famous, make millions of dollars, and move me, my mother, and my sister out of the hood.

When I got my first job out of high school, I saved $300 to record a song, and my brother and I went into the studio. We enjoyed minimal success doing shows at local clubs, but unfortunate situations blocked us from achieving the success we wanted. I eventually became discouraged and gave up on being a recording artist. I thought my purpose was deeply rooted in music, but I just couldn't gain any traction. I felt like I wanted to do music, but music didn't want to do me.

When I became an adult and joined the military, I became a Noncommissioned Officer (NCO). Part of my job as an NCO was to help train and personally develop soldiers. I thoroughly enjoyed helping soldiers train to succeed in their military careers, but also to my surprise, I was good at it. I discovered that I could do what some other leaders couldn't. I could teach in a way that was relatable and memorable to my troops.

Throughout my lifetime, my belief in what my specific purpose is has changed, but my general end purpose is the same as it was in the beginning. My destiny was masked as a doctor, a rapper, and a soldier, but in the end, it still boiled down to helping people. Teaching and motivating them to expand their thinking, and grow into the success that they always dreamed of. Early in life I never thought that I could be an inspiration to anyone, but I slowly came to understand that my history is an example of what can be. We all have the opportunity to leave a mark on this world and influence the masses to embrace their purpose. Will you take advantage of that opportunity?

LIVE YOUR STORY

Have you ever imagined being a cool character in a story? I think we've all seen someone in a movie or two that we wouldn't mind being like, or read a novel that made us wish we could project ourselves into a character's shoes for a while. It's nice to fantasize about living someone else's story, but you have a story that can become more awesome and impactful with each chapter you live.

Do you have a story you tell yourself about how your life is supposed to play out? Unfortunately, most of the stories we tell ourselves are ones where we are born, suffer through a meaningless and painful life, then die. This does not have to be our story. There is no need to suffer. We can turn our lives into romance novels. We can be fearless lead characters, or we can live stories where we thrive and help make the world a better place. But are you willing to live your story? Are you willing to walk an adventurous path and turn yourself into the hero of your own story?

If you are willing to change and grow yourself, your possibilities for success have no end. Just as characters in fictional stories evolve over time, we should all do the same. We should grow from our tribulations, our world views should change, our relationships with family and friends should change for the better, and we should also continually strive for what we want throughout each chapter. The beginning, middle, and end of our stories should be a consistent progression towards a marvelous resolution. If you are determined to create your story of greatness, you can slay dragons, win the heart of the prince or princess, and live your fairytale ending. But whatever you do, make sure that your story is crafted around your purpose.

PURPOSE RECAP

1. Embrace your super powers.

2. Recognize destiny in disguise.

3. Live your story to the fullest.

4. **PINPOINT YOUR LIFE'S PURPOSE.**

Chapter 3
HAVE THE BRAVERY OF A KING

"All our dreams can come true if we have the courage to pursue them"
- WALT DISNEY

I'm sure you've heard the saying the lion is the "king of the jungle". When we think of lions we often view them from this viewpoint, the strong creature that strides purposefully throughout his kingdom. Although the jungle is a dangerous place for most, the lion has no fear. He exudes confidence in who he is, and that confidence is sensed by other animals. The lion is respected as a king, and no other animal dares to attack him for fear of being taken down. Hyenas may bark, and other animals may plot, but capturing and killing a lion is not a task that is easily executed. Lions are not normally hunted, but are instead the beasts that do the hunting.

The lion didn't become king of the jungle by being shy and afraid. He reigned because he was bold, confident, and relentless when pursuing his heart's desire. We need to become lions when we pursue our dreams, and pounce on opportunities as if they were our prey. Many people, like the lion, want to go on the hunt and capture their dreams, but lack follow through due to fear of failure and rejection. What if no one likes my work? What if my business fails? These are common questions people ask themselves when they consider realizing their dreams.

Rather than becoming lions and taking control of their lives, many choose to be gazelles instead. Running in fear as opposed to standing in bravery. Afraid of being eaten alive by society because they blew their chance at success. This is no way to live, and something must be done to turn around this way of thinking.

MAKE YOUR FEARS BACK DOWN

The key to becoming brave in any area of life is quite simple. You must face your phobias if you plan to build your courage. Have you ever done something that you were afraid to do, then noticed afterward that you were not afraid to do it again? Your fear had dissipated because you realized that doing what you feared did not kill you like you thought it might. That's the power of bravery.

Bravery overshadows fear every time. When David battled Goliath, he could have been scared to fight the giant that most people thought would pummel him. But David knew that he was capable of overcoming what seemed to be an insurmountable obstacle.

He hurled his stone and killed that giant. Are you brave enough to do the same? Will you kill what seems to be a dream killer for you? Will you establish dominance and make your fears back down? I hope you will, because your success depends on it!

I once saw a YouTube video where a lion stood on a riverbank face to face with a crocodile. Although the crocodile looked scary and seemed to be a threat, the lion roared in its face with authority, which made the crocodile retreat back into the water.

You can do what that lion did with your fears. You can make fear of failure, rejection, or any other fear back down by exercising your authority like a king, and letting your inner lion roar.

BE BOLD ENOUGH TO BELIEVE

It takes guts to believe in yourself, especially if you've been criticized in the past for attempting to do something your family or friends didn't think you could do. Loved ones may mean well by trying to be realistic about their judgements of your abilities, but you are the only person that is truly aware of your capabilities.

You must be brave enough to inventory your strengths and weaknesses. When you determine the two, you gain a clear picture of what you can do right now, and what you need to work on to broaden your skills for the future. When you are courageous enough to be honest with yourself, you earn the right to walk through the doors of destiny.

An example of being honest with myself about my strengths and weaknesses is knowing that I am strong in the world of writing, but also that I am weak in the realm of procrastination. I am bold enough to believe that I can overcome this weakness because I believe in my power as an overcomer. I believe that weaknesses are temporary setbacks that shrink away as we grow greater belief in ourselves.

When I want to grow my belief in myself and become bold in a certain area of life, there are three tactics that I employ to help turn my weaknesses into strengths. These tactics are as follows:

Gather – I gather as much information as I can about whatever I am trying to accomplish. Whether my research is through reading books, blogs, watching instructional videos, or acquiring knowledge and wisdom from a mentor, I flood my mind with as much information as I can about my chosen subject. This works wonders in helping me feel prepared to tackle any task.

Practice – Once I have gathered all the information I can find, I put everything that I have learned into practice. A good example of this tactic is the time when the alternator went out on my vehicle. I was convinced that I would have to pay someone several hundred dollars to fix the problem. I simply did not believe I knew how to replace the alternator myself. Instead of turning to a mechanic for costly repair, I googled how to replace the alternator and watched instructional videos that showed me what to do step by step. I then put my newfound knowledge into practice and replaced the alternator myself. This saved me a heap of money and grew my confidence in my mechanical skills.

Teach – Teaching others what I have learned and applied in my own life has exponentially improved my belief in myself. Frequent recitation of knowledge and/or doing a task repeatedly makes any skill much easier. As you teach others information or show them how to perform a task, your own level of skill automatically upgrades.

Being bold enough to believe in ourselves and acquiring the necessary skills to grow our confidence is critical to our success. If we cower in the corner when we are faced with challenges, we will never be able to ascend to those higher heights that are reserved for the bold and brave.

OVERTHINKING IS OVERRATED

Have you ever heard the term study long study wrong? Many people study so long that they talk themselves out of taking action. They overthink their ambitions, which leads to underachievement.

Overthinking is one of the biggest enemies of bravery. Just when you start to feel confident about achieving your goals, overthinking rears its ugly head and robs you of your motivation. The longer you question whether or not a situation will work out in your favor, the more you empower this enemy.

I have missed out on many opportunities in the past due to overthinking. I have been guilty of obsessing over what could go wrong instead of getting excited about what could go right. Too much negative thinking can create self -fulfilling prophecies. If you think you are going to underperform on a project and those thoughts stick in your mind, then that will become your reality. Your thoughts shape your world.

Your mind feasts on whatever you feed it. If you feed it negative thoughts, those thoughts manifest in the form of fear and anxiety. Fears grow within the darkness of pessimism, while courage grows within the light of optimism. The next time you notice you are overthinking and wallowing in what can go wrong, reverse your thinking, and replace it with a positive mental picture.

See yourself getting that pat on the back from your boss instead of being chewed out for messing up.

Most times when we overthink things, we create negative scenarios in our minds that will probably not even happen. We worry unnecessarily and get stuck in inaction for fear of an undesirable outcome. We also inevitably end up wasting time worrying about what could have been. Time is valuable. You can never go back and reclaim your time...no matter what current memes and social media jokes try to tell you. Once you waste an hour worrying about what if, that hour is gone forever. You must learn to use your time wisely as it is a valuable, yet fleeting resource that waits for no one.

Establish the habit of thinking good thoughts. Positive thought leads to positive action. When you envision perfect performance and favorable results, you act in accordance with your vision. Your newfound confidence will grow and set you up to take on any obstacle that dares to stand before you.

ARE YOU AFRAID OF SUCCESS?

It may sound silly, but some people are afraid of success. Why would anyone fear something that they want so bad? The truth is that they fear the things that come along with achieving their goals and dreams, and not the dream itself. They want the effects of having high prestige and millions of dollars, but they're afraid that they can't execute the causes that create the results they seek. I know this because I used to be one of those people. I used to look at successful people and think I would love to live that life, while subconsciously being afraid to try and change my reality. Here are some reasons that I was once afraid to pursue success:

1. Fear of Change

I have always been a creature of habit. Once I was settled into a certain life pattern, it was always a challenge for me to change. This challenge was eliminated for me when I realized that without change there can be no growth, and without growth there can be no success. So, I became accustomed to change. I got comfortable with doing things that I wouldn't normally do. For instance, I used to hate reading. I thought it took too long and I had a problem with retaining what I had read. I eventually came to the realization that reading could be the bridge between me and my success. Reading about other people's thoughts and experiences could help provide the insight I needed to change for the better. I found the value in reading which made it more palatable. Over time, I learned to be okay with reading slow, which helped me to retain more of the information I consumed.

By learning to embrace change, you will empower yourself to become better. You will unleash the genius inside of you that won't be satisfied until you have reached your full potential. Will you embrace change so that you may achieve excellence? Will you break through the wall of mediocrity that is holding you back? If you do, then your determination will be the sledgehammer that enables you to pound your way through. Don't be afraid of change, because it could mean the difference between your success and failure.

2. All Eyes on Me

I am an introvert by nature. I have always been quiet until getting to know people, and it has always felt weird having attention focused on me. I used to avoid public speaking for those exact reasons. Wondering what people were thinking of me as they seemed to stare into my naked soul. This was a huge barrier that impeded my route to success. I learned to overcome this by shifting my thoughts. I stopped wondering what people were thinking of me, and realized that through confident body language and tonality, I had the power to influence what they thought of me.

I also found that when you speak confidently on the subject matter that you present, your audience is more focused on the content than on you. You can sound more confident by knowing your subject matter inside and out. Study and practice your presentation as often as possible, so that presenting the information becomes second nature for you.

The first time I gave a business presentation, my business coach spoke before I did. I saw that he was confident and well spoken, he shared personal stories pertaining to the service we were selling, and he had no problem with people staring at him as he spoke. As a result, we received at least one sale at the end of the presentation due to his fearless speech. I was amazed at how good he was at talking in front of people, and this inspired me to pursue public speaking skills that would knock the socks off my audiences.

3. Fear of Making Mistakes

Over the years, I have grown to learn that mistakes are the greatest success tools known to man. I used to be afraid to make mistakes, because I feared embarrassment. Once I gained a certain level of success, I never wanted to be regarded as a fool for doing something wrong. But making mistakes along your journey allows you to assess where you went wrong, regroup your thoughts, and create a better strategy for doing things.

I once invited some people in my neighborhood to a business gathering at my house by placing flyers in their mailboxes. I thought this would surely draw a crowd. I bought snacks and drinks, and set up all the necessary equipment to present with. When 6:00 pm rolled around, not one soul showed up. I felt sad and defeated at that moment. I told my business coach what happened, and he told me instead of putting flyers in mailboxes I should have knocked on doors, smiled and introduced myself, and personally invited my prospects to the event.

Through that mistake, I found that personal interaction is better than leaving a flyer in a mailbox. Had I not made this mistake I would have never learned the lesson. We all can learn what we should do by first doing what we should not do. Don't be afraid to make mistakes, because each lesson you learn along the way will help move you one step closer to success.

RECAP OF BRAVERY

1. Make your fears back down.

2. Be bold enough to believe in yourself.

3. Stop overthinking every little thing.

4. Don't be afraid to succeed in life.

5. **HAVE THE BRAVERY OF A KING.**

Chapter 4
BEWARE OF NEGATIVE SELF TALK

"It's not what you say out of your mouth that determines your life, it's what you whisper to yourself that has the most power"
- ROBERT KIYOSAKI

If you saw a person walking down the street talking to their self, out loud for all the world to hear... would you think they were crazy? I probably would, especially if I heard them carrying on a conversation as if someone else was there. Well, even though most of us are perfectly sane, we talk to ourselves daily. We repeatedly tell ourselves what we can and cannot do. What is and is not possible for us. This practice can either be used to build us up or tear us down when pursuing our dreams.

Many people internalize negative talk from others to the point that they convince themselves that their goals can't be achieved. They literally sabotage their own success by thinking to themselves, maybe that person is right. Maybe I don't have what it takes to manifest my vision. Maybe I shouldn't think big because all my past achievements in life have been small. No one else in my family has done anything significant, so what makes me any different?

What we must realize is that most people that are not confident in their own abilities, transfer their thoughts of inferiority and self-doubt onto others. Since they can't see a way to do what they want to do in life, they try to block your view of your goals. These people must be avoided if you plan to progress toward your destiny. Miracles can be achieved in your life if you only have faith in possibilities.

SPEAK LIFE TO YOURSELF

Whenever negative thoughts enter your mind, tell yourself to STOP. Interrupt that thought pattern by mentally yelling at yourself and replacing your negative thoughts with positive ones.

For instance, if you think that you are unworthy of success, stop that thought immediately and tell yourself that you are more than worthy and deserve every good thing that is coming to you. Redirecting the conversation with yourself from negative to positive is a powerful technique for getting your thinking back on the right track.

I have had to use this tactic many times to counter my own negative thoughts. I once thought to myself, you're just a nobody with a poor background. You're not qualified to help anyone or rise above your own past situations. I countered by telling myself that it doesn't matter where I'm from or what my past is. I am a great success with a bright future. I have the knowledge and wisdom to help people move past stagnancy, and progress into better living.

Many people view their past as a stumbling block that disqualifies them from teaching others to move forward in life. On the contrary, your past is a stepping stone that qualifies you to teach others, because life experience has been your greatest teacher. Speak life and positivity to yourself, and believe you can do whatever you put your mind to, because you can.

TALK THE TALK AND RUN THE RUN

When I was in the Army, we used to do a two-mile run as part of our physical fitness test. I was never a really a good runner, but I always seemed to pass the test. The reason I passed wasn't because I didn't get tired during the run. Like everyone else, I became winded and tired while running, but what helped me pass the test was my self-talk. I talked myself across the finish line. I made myself believe I was an elite runner on the track, and that nothing could stop me. While my back hurt and my legs were weak, I spoke the opposite of what I felt.

I told myself that my back felt great and my legs were strong. Repeating these phrases to myself made me believe them, and I felt like a thoroughbred horse. I even talked to God on the run. I said, "Lord, help me on this run. I belong to you. If I fail, you fail. And I know you can't fail." When I spoke this way, my second wind seemed to kick in and give me the needed strength to push through those two miles.

SILENCE THE CRITIC

There's a critical voice in your head that likes to list all the reasons that you're not good enough to do what you want to do. It will tell you that you don't have experience, you don't know the right people, you're not smart enough, or success is reserved for everyone except you. You need to silence this voice, and here's how you do it.

1. Meditate on the Good

When the voice of doom and gloom begins whispering its negative opinions to you, meditate on those moments when you did something great. Remember a time when that voice said you were incapable of doing something, but you did it anyway. Think back to one of those times when you beat the odds, and boosted your confidence through bold action and unexpected accomplishment.

47

The negative voice in your head is not the deciding authority for what you can achieve in life. It only has as much power over you as you allow it to have. You are fully in charge of your world, and no outside influence or inside voice can dictate limitations for you. Meditate on those things that you have done right frequently, and you will inevitably clear your mind of the negative voice that holds you back.

2. Imperfections Don't Define You

Most people are bothered when they think about their imperfections. This attitude towards your shortcomings feeds your negative voice with ammunition to shoot you down at will. You can disarm the critic by embracing imperfections. By removing the self-imposed expectation of perfection in your life, you will free yourself from the sting of criticism. If you are okay with not firing off perfect answers in your next job interview, not performing every detail perfectly in the workplace, or not hiring the perfect candidate for the job, you will find that the negative voice in your head begins to go silent.

3. Know Thyself

Knowing yourself makes it hard for criticism to affect you. When you know within your core that you are awesome, your emotions become bulletproof and your inner critic becomes your inner cheerleader. Get familiar with your strengths and capitalize on them by further cultivating and growing them to the level of mastery. This may take some time. It may take several weeks, months, or years, but it will be well worth the time investment. Knowing and bettering yourself solidifies a positive self-evaluation towards yourself, and nullifies the opinion of the critic within.

THE ANGEL AND THE DEVIL

We all have two voices that speak to us on a regular basis. We have the voice of the angel (optimism) and the voice of the devil (pessimism). The angel speaks positivity over our lives by telling us that we are worthy and capable of getting all the good things that life can offer us, as well as being whatever we choose to be. If we listen to the angel, its influence will be magnified in our hearts and minds. It will eventually consume our thoughts and ultimately drive us into taking positive actions.

On the other hand, the devil speaks negativity in our ear. He tells us that we can't be and do what we want, and that we will never amount to much of anything. He wants each of us to fail and live a life of mediocrity, doubt, and unhappiness, when we should choose to accept truth. The truth is that we are masters of our own fates, instead of victims of our circumstances.

We have the power to change what we don't like in our lives. If we want to lose weight, we can diet and exercise to lose the pounds.

If we want to switch careers, we can take classes or study books to learn the necessary skills. If we want to be in a relationship, we can work to become the type of person we want to attract. It's up to us to determine who we will listen to. I urge you to listen to the voice of the angel in your ear. It always has your best interest in mind, and would love nothing more than to see you succeed in life. Drown out the devil's voice. Focus on the voice of optimism and positivity. Allow it to become louder and louder until it is all that you can hear.

RECAP OF SELF TALK

1. Always speak life to yourself.

2. Talk the talk and run the run.

3. Silence your inner critic.

4. Listen to the angel in your ear, not the devil.

5. **BEWARE OF NEGATIVE SELF TALK.**

Chapter 5
THE POWER OF DOING

"Action is the foundational key to all success"
-PABLO PICASSO

Millions worldwide make New Year's resolutions every year claiming that they will make a change for the better in one or more areas of their lives. These changes include the following:

1. Lose weight
2. Start their own business
3. Save more money
4. Quit smoking
5. Quit drinking

Some say that they don't have time to get to the gym like they said they would, and some claim they are still waiting for the right time to quit their dead-end job and start their own business. The bottom line is that these are excuses. You can make time for what is important to you, and there is no "right time" to dive into a new and life altering endeavor. The closest you will ever get to the right time is called RIGHT NOW. When you stop talking about making things happen and move towards getting it done. But how does one do this? How does one go from being a procrastinator to being a productive agent of action? Here are the keys.

1. Write a To-Do List

To-do lists are some of the most powerful tools for inspiration. We all need a shot of motivation if we plan to be productive. Coffee drives many people into action in the morning, but a good to-do list can be just as effective. When we have a written image of what we need to get done in front of us, this sends a signal to our brain that sparks a desire for action. Our motivation to act is driven by our desire to erase as many tasks as possible from the to-do list. Removing tasks from the list gives us a sense of great achievement. When we make progress, we want to continue making progress for as long as possible. These lists have worked wonders for me in the past, and I am confident that they will do the same for you, if you choose to try them.

2. Little Beginnings

Undergoing big tasks can be rather intimidating. When we think of the energy it will take to execute, it can leave us feeling overwhelmed. That's why we should start small. Knock out the smaller tasks that are easily accomplished and work our way up to bigger things.

I relate this concept to working out in the gym. When we start a workout routine for the first time, we don't go in expecting to lift 300 pounds in the first few days. We start with a much lighter weight, and gradually work our way up to the heavier weight. If we were to try lifting 300 pounds on the first day, we would be crushed under the pressure. The same holds true for our goals.

We must take it slow and build our confidence and strength before attempting to take on large scale projects, or else the pressure would have the potential to crush us as soon as we start. The skill of doing is one that must be developed like a muscle. The more you work to build it, the bigger this muscle becomes. Before you know it, you will be able to handle big tasks and goals, simply because you decided to start small.

3. Focus on the Prize

Pondering on the reward you will receive after completing a task can be just the nudge you need to get things started. When my wife and I want our children to work hard for better grades in school we take away something that they want, which is usually their cell phones, video games, or television privileges. This causes them to take massive action in their classes. They study more, take notes, and even go to tutoring if they need to. The reason they are willing to do these things is because their eye is on a prize. They have something to gain if they put forth the effort.

Employees in the workforce also respond well to reward. A substandard employee may be inspired to take greater action if he/she knows that they will be promoted or receive a raise due to extra effort. They may also be inspired to work harder if they know that they may be terminated unless they increase their performance. Their prize for increased performance would be avoiding a meeting with Human Resources one Friday afternoon.

What do you have to gain from making things happen? What reward is waiting for you on the other side of a diligent effort? Exploring the answers to these questions may be the shovel that helps unearth your motivation. Identify your prize and develop ways to keep it before you so that you can remain motivated to make things happen!

KNOWING VS. DOING

Many of us have knowledge of what we need to do to make our lives better, yet we just don't do it. We may have been told for years that knowledge is power, but this is a myth. Knowledge is potential power. This power could be compared to potential energy, which is stored energy. Energy or knowledge that is only stored or unused is worthless. It can be likened to a product in a store sitting on the shelf collecting dust. It could make money for the storeowner if it is sold, but if it stays on the shelf, the seller reaps no benefit. Your mind is a storehouse filled with valuable knowledge that could be of use to you and many others if only you were willing to unleash its power.

Energy that is in motion is called kinetic energy. We all grow our kinetic energy through doing. By getting the ball rolling, we create a snowball effect that compounds small efforts into big results. But that energy/power can never be created if we sit on our knowledge without putting it in motion through ACTION.

We can never complain about our circumstances if we are able to do something to change them, but choose not to. This disqualifies us from our right to complain to others that we never have enough money, that our marriage is going downhill, or that we always seem to catch bad breaks in life. We can move on our ideas now, and completely change the trajectories of our lives. It might not be easy to do at first because we live happily in our comfort zones, but with practice we can create habits for ourselves that become the building blocks for empires.

YOUR SUCCESS AIN'T GONNA CREATE ITSELF

If you plan to get things done in your life you must be willing to do the work. You must be willing to put aside entertainment such as Facebook, Instagram, TV shows, and other things that do not help move you closer to achieving your desired results.

Grow Into Success

Think of your goals like a game of football. In this game, the objective is to move the ball forward until you reach the end zone and score points. During the game, there are linebackers that try to keep the opposing team from reaching the end zone. You must have a plan in place to maneuver around these linebackers so you can reach the other end of the field. The running back may run the ball a certain number of yards to advance the ball forward, or the quarterback may pass to a receiver. With each run or pass, sometimes the attempt is successful and sometimes it's not, but the team keeps trying until they finally score. After repeating these actions tirelessly throughout the game, the team that moves the ball forward into the end zone the most times wins.

Your pursuit of success is the same way. You must take actions that move you towards the end zone (your goal) every day. There will be linebackers (setbacks) such as doubts and fears, that may slow you down along the way, but you can't let these setbacks stop you. You must make plans to side step those setbacks and reach your goals anyway. After you do the work of moving forward in action on a regular basis, you score enough points to win the game. You put yourself in position to be holding the trophy in the end. Imagine the confetti falling and the crowd cheering for you, because you never gave up. You worked hard to obtain the victory that would have otherwise eluded you. The actions you take today create the successes of your tomorrow. Put in the work and start creating today.

DO DIFFERENT TO GET DIFFERENT

I grew up in New Orleans, LA where a lot of people I knew and grew up with had negative attitudes. As unhappy as many of them were with their life situations, they always refused to do something different. I decided to leave my hometown and join the Army when I was 26 years old. This was a major culture shock for me in the beginning because I had never traveled or lived outside of Louisiana or Mississippi. I attended boot camp at Ft. Jackson, SC., where my comfort zone was totally obliterated. I was forced to go to sleep early and wake up at ungodly times of the morning. I was forced to take orders from barking drill sergeants, and to learn things that were completely foreign to me. This was the most frustrating, yet life changing nine weeks of my life.

By going to bed and waking up early, I learned discipline. By learning to be a good follower, I learned to be a good leader. By acquiring skills that were foreign to me, I realized my capacity for personal growth. I learned that there was a vastly different and beautiful world outside of where I grew up that was just waiting for me to discover it.

Since moving away from New Orleans, I have been able to improve my financial situation, buy a new home, meet my wonderful wife while deployed to Iraq, and meet great friends from all over the world. Would I have had most of these opportunities had I stayed in New Orleans? Probably not. I would probably be living a life of negativity like a lot of the people I grew up with. I am happy to have done something different, because it has allowed me to change the course of my life forever. Will you do something different to get different results?

<u>RECAP OF DOING</u>

1. Take action on what you know to do.

2. You have to create your own success first.

3. Do different to get different results.

4. **THERE'S POWER IN DOING.**

Chapter 6
WILLPOWER IS THE WAY

"Those that are firm in their will mold the world to themselves"
-JOHANN VON GOETHE

How strong is the human will? What can be accomplished by wielding an iron will? Surely anyone who has had to force themselves out of a warm bed, away from the dinner table, or away from the television to study has experienced the will in action. It's not always easy to push yourself in certain situations, but here are some practices that can increase your chances of imposing your will when the need arises.

1. Sleep Like a Baby

Proper rest is one of the main ingredients for strong willpower. When our brains are fatigued, our will becomes weak. We often rule against doing what we should do, and opt to do something that requires no mental or physical energy.

When we get a good night's rest, our brains are recharged. We wake up in the morning feeling mentally and physically refreshed, and ready to take on the day. There may be times when it is difficult to get that much needed shut eye, but here are a few tips that should help you drift into dreamland.

- ❖ **Reading** – Exercising your mind with some light reading before bed can make you mentally fatigued.
- ❖ **Limit Your Drinks** – Avoid drinking anything close to bedtime, especially caffeine. This will keep you from being wired and reduce bathroom trips.
- ❖ **Stay Cool** – Rest is hard to find when the room is hot. Keep your room at a cool temperature for a good slumber.
- ❖ **Dark and Quiet** – Turn off any light or noise making devices before bed. They may cause an active brain and open eyes.

I have tried these techniques in the past, and they've worked for me. Try them for yourself and see if they help you rest peacefully through the night.

2. Weigh the Pros and Cons

Ask yourself what are the positives and negatives associated with getting a task done. A positive result may be that you get to take your dream vacation if you save a certain amount of money in 6 months. That could motivate you to go in to work when you feel like taking the day off.

A negative consequence may be that you lose a very lucrative contract at work because you weren't properly prepared for a presentation. You didn't have the will to research and organize your information like you should have, which caused you to miss out on a wonderful opportunity.

Analyze the pros and cons concerning your willpower. When you feel lazy, think of the best and worst case scenarios that could result from executing or slacking off. This could be the deciding factor as to whether you perform your most crucial tasks or not.

3. Modify Your Mood

Sometimes a change in your mood can make all the difference in your performance. You may feel angry, lazy, undervalued, or incapable at times, but there are ways to modify your mood on command. Try these.

❖ **Listening to Music** – They say music calms the savage beast, but I say music modifies the mood of a man/woman. When you find that a bad mood hinders your performance, play some songs that inspire you or sing them in your head.

❖ **Gratitude** – Thinking of what you are thankful for also has a mood boosting effect. It's hard to be thankful and sad or angry simultaneously.

❖ **Watch Motivational Videos** – This one has been a lifesaver for me. Watching videos that encourage you to be great can be quite uplifting. These can be found on YouTube and other websites.

We have all let our moods get the best of us at one time or another. It's important to understand that we can't stay in that place. We must move past the bad mood if we are to make good things happen. So, get up, dust yourself off, and go get 'em!

4. Avoid All Distractions

Distractions can be the main source of derailment when we are on track to get stuff done. We can be knocked out of our zone and struggle to get back to business simply because the phone rang. Here are some tips to help keep you from being sabotaged by outside forces when striving for productivity.

❖ **Clear the Clutter** – a messy desk or work area can scatter your attention all over the place. Put away the things you don't need to create a distraction free work environment.

❖ **Kill Your Phone** – Putting your phone on vibrate isn't good enough, because you will still hear it buzz. Turn it off or turn on airplane mode to ensure a distraction free work session.

❖ **Move to Your Zen Spot** – Family and friends can be serious distractions when you are trying to be productive. Find a quiet place away from the noise and chaos to maximize your focus.

❖ **Be an Early Bird** – Getting up early is a fantastic way to get work done. When your family is asleep, it's prime time for knocking out some of your most important tasks.

Avoiding distractions can be your best defense against a lack of willpower. Employ this tactic as a time management tool as well as a method to keep your work flow going.

5. Stick to Your Guns

Temptation has a way of making us deviate from our well laid plans, so we must have a strategy in place when it creeps up on us. Decide up front that you will stick to your plan no matter what. Think about the momentum you will lose if you put your plan on the back burner. In the past when I've made plans to do things, but didn't execute due to lack of will, I felt like a total loser. I felt like I wasn't in control of my actions. To avoid this feeling, you must convince yourself to stay diligent in the face of temptation before the temptation occurs. This will help build your willpower in ways you can't even imagine.

Lyndell Johnson

WILLPOWER OVER WON'T POWER

When I graduated from high school back in the mid 90's, I decided not to go to college. I felt that I had suffered enough and opted to join the work force. Throughout the following seven years I worked as a grocery store employee, a mall janitor, a restaurant dishwasher, a dock worker in a warehouse, and an order picker for Coca Cola. I earned an average living from these jobs, but I was still missing a sense of purpose and wanted a better life for me and my family, so I joined the military.

I served ten years in the Army and was proud of the value I had contributed to the organization. There were many early mornings and late nights on the job, but I felt that the sacrifice was worth it. With three deployments to Iraq and Afghanistan under my belt, I became burnt out and missed my family terribly, so I decided to leave the military life behind. What would be my next move?

I decided to go back to school, which was a scary decision for me because I had been out of school for the past eighteen years. I was in my late thirties, and had basically brain dumped most of what I learned in school. I would be starting over from almost ground zero. I asked myself if I could pull it off, and wondered if I had the will to endure four years of college for a degree in Business Management. I didn't know for sure whether I was able, but nonetheless I was going for it.

Grow Into Success

After applying to college, I received a letter saying that I needed to write an entrance essay explaining why the school should accept me. I hadn't written an essay in almost two decades, and had no idea how to format a paper. I enlisted my wife, who was also in college at the time, to help me with formatting. I felt bad for needing help writing a paper, and hoped the day would come when I no longer needed it.

Anyone who has attended college understands how writing intensive it can be. Writing essays seems to be the cornerstone of the college curriculum. I had to write an essay on my first day in class, but I at least felt a tad bit better about it after the entrance essay. One of my first courses was called Communications Essentials. This class provided some writing guidelines and gave me increased confidence in my writing ability. Before I knew it, I was receiving high grades on most of my papers. I hoped I would eventually become a better writer, but I never expected to get good grades and great feedback on my work. This was a definite win!

The moral of this story is that willpower is a vital component of growth that can help lead you to success in your chosen field. Had I told myself I won't be able to go back to college or I won't write the entrance essay, I probably wouldn't have learned to write on my own. I also wouldn't have had enough confidence and drive to write this book. Having the will to go back to school surely put me on the path towards learning to run my own business and learning the necessary skills to help others.

Do away with "won't power" and your willpower will shine through. Call on your higher self to rise to the occasion and fulfill your potential when you are intimidated by your aspirations. Remember that no goal is too hard or too big for you to accomplish. Whether you want to be the CEO of a Fortune 500 company, a bestselling author, or a better parent to your children, you can do whatever you want. At the end of the day, you must make this simple decision. Either you will do the work to make your dreams come true, or you won't.

RECAP OF WILLPOWER

1. Understand that willpower is a prerequisite for success.

2. Choose willpower over "won't power".

3. Will yourself to work toward your greatness.

4. **KNOW THAT WILLPOWER IS THE WAY.**

Chapter 7
SEE YOURSELF AS A ROCKSTAR

"Reality is based on perception"
-GEOFF THOMPSON

How do you see yourself? When you look in the mirror, do you see an underdog or an overcomer? Do you see an awesome person with talents and gifts to contribute to this world, or just a nobody merely existing while time marches on? Your perception of who and what you are can be a humungous gamechanger in your life. If you don't see yourself as valuable and worthy, I'm going to help you change that in this chapter.

Many people that are currently considered to be stars in their industries didn't start out that way. Several big named actors, singers, athletes, and CEOs grew up poor with negative outlooks on their futures. Some grew up in broken homes, some were homeless for many years, some were ridiculed for being different, and some even had learning disabilities, but they saw something in themselves that inspired them to keep chasing their dreams.

In my teenage years, I was labeled as a misfit. During my high school years, I was perceived as a nerd with a horrible acne problem. The way I was treated made me feel like less than nothing. I had no direction in life, and no one to encourage me and help build my self-esteem. As a result, I pretty much kept to myself and was anti-social for many years. It wasn't until I graduated high school and joined the work force that I began to see myself differently.

I once worked for a shipping and receiving company loading trucks overnight. I was young and full of energy back then, in my early twenties, so my team and I loaded trucks at what seemed to be lightning speed. Supervisors praised us for our productivity, and for the first time in my life, I truly felt valued. I felt like I was accepted and belonged to a team. That job marked the death of a pimple faced nerd and the birth of a ROCK STAR.

EMULATE THE GREATS

I don't know about you, but when I was a kid I wanted to be like the rock stars. I thought people like Axle Rose, David Lee Roth, and other rockers were the coolest people ever. They were famous, had lots of money, and were at the top of their games when they performed. These greats had certain tactics they could attribute their massive successes to, and many of those tactics could be implemented by anyone willing to put forth the effort. Some of those tactics are as follows:

1. Build Your Celebrity

If you want to be a rock star in life, you must create your own celebrity status. You must have unwavering faith in your own gifts and talents, and promote yourself shamelessly. It doesn't matter how you do it. You could promote yourself through social media, newspaper ads, TV commercials, networking like crazy, or hiring a PR specialist. The bottom line is that if nobody knows you, it will be impossible to be a rock star in life.

For instance, many self-published authors have become famous by promoting their own books first. They proved themselves marketable and in demand before becoming titans in the publishing and film industries. E.L. James was self-published before receiving a traditional publishing deal for Fifty Shades of Grey. She created her fanbase and attracted mainstream publishers' interest after creating her own massive following. You can do the same by making an extraordinary effort to establish your own rock star status in whatever your field may be.

2. Find Passion in Your Purpose

Passion is one of the main forces that drives the rock star lifestyle. This is what allows you to pursue your purpose without succumbing to adversity. If you truly enjoy what you do, nothing can stop you from partaking in that activity. Setbacks are inconsequential when you are pushed by passion, and instead of seeing your work as a pain you see it as a pleasure. Work and fun merge into one when passion is applied to your craft.

When you are passionate about what you do, you become energized while doing it. When rock stars perform on stage, they literally come to life. They are so filled with passion during their performances that they have been known to dive off stage into crowds of people. That's how you must be in your career or business. You must be so fired up that your enthusiasm rubs off on everyone around you. If you are not passionate about what you do, you should make a conscious effort to find at least one aspect of your work that sparks your flame. Figure out what makes you tick and focus your efforts around that one thing. Before you know it, you'll be rocking and rolling like Jimi Hendrix.

3. Expand Your Vision

Many people focus on the wrong visions for their lives. They focus on visions of the past rather than visions for their

73

future. They determine that they can never become great, because their early lives were tough. They still see themselves as that poor kid that got teased in school, or that kid that felt unloved because their parents were never around due to work obligations.

If you look at the lives of successful people, many of their beginnings in life and career were less than desirable. Oprah Winfrey grew up in the small farming community of Kosciusko, Mississippi where family friends and relatives sexually abused her. Former Starbucks CEO Howard Shultz grew up in housing projects of Brooklyn, New York, and Harry Potter author, J.K. Rowling was once a single mother on welfare and even tried committing suicide when she was broke and depressed.

What do these three super achievers have in common? None of them allowed their earlier life situations to handicap their minds. They didn't let visions of their past stop them from expanding their visions for future success.

Where is your focus directed? How big is your vision for your dream? If you are focused on the pain of your past, I urge you to redirect your focus to the future. Shift and expand your vision onto a larger playing field. You could very well be the next iconic figure in your industry, but if you can't see it you will never be it.

4. Learn to Leap Again

When I was a kid we use to play a game called leap frog where someone would squat down with their hands on their knees, and another person would run behind them and leap over their back. As kids, we were never afraid that something bad would happen while playing this game, we would just leap without fear.

As adults, we become afraid of leaping. We perceive it as a risk of being hurt. If we plan to harness our full potential and reap the greatest benefits in life, we must be comfortable with taking risks. We must learn to see the possibilities instead of the problems associated with risk. Everything in life is a risk, including life itself. When we wake up in the morning, we never have the guarantee of living the entire day, but we move forward anyway. When we propose to our spouses, we run the risk of being rejected. When we board airplanes, we risk crashing and burning during the flight. When we drive our cars, we risk dying in an accident. And when we gamble, we risk parting with our precious and hard-earned money. Why is that? It's because these are all things that we are comfortable doing since we do them so often, or we feel they are necessary activities that help facilitate our happiness in some way. We must get to a point where discomfort is the new normal. The reason most people are deathly afraid of public speaking is because of the risk of embarrassment. Little do they know, the ability to speak in front of a crowd could be the very skill they need to revolutionize their lives.

So, don't be afraid to leap. Don't be afraid of taking risks. Many successful entrepreneurs are only where they are because they took a chance on themselves. The next time you feel hesitant about taking a risk that could benefit you, remember that champions never win if they never take the risk of losing.

5. Never Give Up

No matter what happens on your journey in life, never give up. Never give adversity the satisfaction of defeating you. You have a power inside of you that enables you to keep going when your mind tells you to quit. Harness that power and prove yourself to be the warrior that you are. Tough times will come that seem to literally knock the wind out of you, but when that happens you must hear the bell ring in your head, go into your corner, recompose yourself, and come out swinging.

Beat down those walls that attempt to hold you back. Wrap your head around the concept of making persistence a part of your lifestyle. If your goal is to increase sales by $10,000 this month, be consistent in your efforts. If you don't reach your goal this month, don't pull back…push harder. Light a fire underneath yourself and jump into action that will ensure your victory. When the smoke clears and the dust settles, I want you to look back at life with no regrets. Deny yourself the ability to say I gave up on myself, by going after what you want today. You will surely harvest the spoils of war if you never give up.

ROCK STAR ROYALTY

Mick Jagger is arguably one of the greatest rock stars of all time. His musical performances with The Rolling Stones are legendary and would suggest that he has been a rocker his entire life. Nothing could be further from the truth. Mick Jagger attended the London School of Economics, which is far from performing arts, but he left school to form the band with guitarist Keith Richards.

Even though Mick Jagger was an economics student early on, he didn't see himself as an economics student. He saw himself as a rock star. He believed he was a performer and that was what he became. The Rolling Stones had many major hits in the music industry, but if Mick had limited himself to just being an economics student, we would have never had the pleasure of experiencing one of the most prolific rock bands in music history.

Like Mick Jagger, you may be part of an industry that is totally unrelated to being a rock star. You may work in finance, management, marketing, or own a small business. In any case, you can still be a rock star. Maybe not one that graces stages all over the world, but a rock star in your industry of choice. All you need is a stellar attitude and work ethic to help rank you among the greatest rock stars that ever walked this earth.

ROCK STAR RECAP

1. Emulate the greats that came before you.

2. Expand your vision of your future.

3. Never give up.

4. Follow Mick Jagger's example of right perception.

5. **SEE YOURSELF AS A ROCK STAR**.

Chapter 8
EVOLVE THROUGH EDUCATION

"The roots of education are bitter, but the fruit is sweet"
-ARISTOTLE

We've all heard that we should get an education, so we can someday get a decent job and live the American dream by purchasing a nice car and house with a white picket fence. When most of us think about education, we think about classrooms, teachers, writing essays, math homework, and other school related items. Although these are common components of traditional education, formal colleges and universities are not the only pathways to learning.

Personal Development speaker Jim Rohn once stated, "Formal education will make you a living, self-education will make you a fortune." This is such a true statement, because many of the most successful people in business either dropped out of college or never attended. I am not opposed to formal education, because some professions absolutely require it, but you can still become wildly successful without racking up tens of thousands of dollars in college debt. Here are some ways to expand your intellect on your own.

1. Practice Thinking

We are all capable of thinking, but how often do you set time aside to focus on strategy? Have you ever thought about where you want to be, then mapped out the route you must take to get there? Thinking is a primary requirement for success. Action is secondary. Since we were all born with this standard piece of equipment called a brain, we must practice utilizing it if we plan to craft a life filled with meaning.

Our thoughts are seeds that must be watered for growth to take place. How do we water these seeds? We take time to intentionally mold them by practicing stillness, because this busy and noisy world we live in has a way of drowning out our thoughts. We must bask in silence and focus our energy on life changing ideas. Ideas that when acted upon could make us millionaires. Ideas that when acted upon will change who we are now into the best versions of ourselves. If you decide to cultivate the habit of thinking and brainstorming ideas, your seeds/thoughts will soon blossom into a beautiful life of enjoyment.

2. Become People Smart

Most things that you want in life will come as a result of your relationships with other people. As much as many of us would like to do so, it is virtually impossible to achieve extraordinary levels of success based solely on our own efforts. You must be able to get along with your boss if you want a promotion. Likewise, you must be able to get along with team members for joint assignments, and you must be likable to sell to your customers. No one jumps to buy products from the sleazy sales guy because people typically do business with those that they like and trust.

People are portals to the world you want to live in. Getting along with others and learning to see things from their perspectives are some of the most valuable skills you can have. For example, you may see your boss as a jerk, but have you ever asked yourself why he/she comes off as a jerk? Maybe they are feeling overwhelmed by pressure from upper management, therefore they feel they must be hard on employees in order to get results. As an employee, a manager, a parent, or anyone trying to get positive results from other people, you must be empathetic enough to understand where they are coming from. People usually aren't eager to jump to follow the instructions of those who don't make an effort to understand their point of view. Show them you care.

3. Invest in Your Intentions

Whatever your intention is, you must be willing to invest something into it. You must decide if you will invest your time, money, or effort into what you intend to do, but you must sow if you plan to reap a return. You may invest your time by volunteering for a worthy cause if your intention is to make a difference in the lives of others such as the homeless or other groups in need of assistance. You may invest your money into courses and training if your intention is to make yourself more skilled and valuable in the marketplace. Or you can invest your efforts if your intention is to invent a product that will solve a problem for the masses.

Just like investing in the stock market yields a return, so does investing in your intentions. Time, money, and effort are the currencies that can help grow your portfolio of dreams. By sacrificing these things that mean the most to you, you open a gateway to a greater life. Not only do you work towards a better future, but you work towards a better you. By becoming a person that is willing to grow through personal investment, even if you lose all that you have, you will be able to recover all that was lost because of who you have become.

4. Draw a Better Circle

There is a saying that if you are the smartest person in your circle, you need to find a new circle. I find this to be so true. By associating yourself with friends that are more knowledgeable than you, you gradually upgrade your intellect. It's like iron sharpening iron, but you must separate yourself from the bad circle first. I think you know who the bad circle is. Those friends that would rather talk gossip than talk business. The ones that are like anchors pulling you down, rather than helping hands that pull you up. This is the circle that you should avoid like the plague.

To draw a better circle, you must first make yourself attractive. You must be sharp to attract the interest of sharp individuals. They must see something in you that they can identify with. High achievers are not interested in associating with low achievers. If you are a low achiever that is only interested in playing video games and engaging in senseless activities, I urge you to change your behavior. Read articles and books that feed your mind, so you can join in on the conversations of the circle you intend to join. You must be relatable in order to create relationships with people that can help you grow intellectually.

THE READING REVOLUTION

"Reading is fundamental" has been a popular phrase for as long as I can remember. I personally believe it is the cornerstone of learning, and a mandatory component of any success plan. Schools issue books to students because they understand that reading is the

way to imprint ideas and information into the student's mind. Through reading, one can live an adventure through fiction novels or learn to be the next groundbreaking tech expert in the ever-changing field of Computer Science. Books can inspire dreams and teach us the necessary skills to bring those dreams to fruition, but we must be willing to read.

In this age of Facebook, Snapchat, Twitter, and other social media platforms, many people are more drawn to watching and making funny videos, twerk videos, and videos of people fighting in the street than anything else. In no way do these videos advance their lives in the direction they should go, but it is what's popular in this day and time. I personally prefer to watch videos that teach me how to do things that can save or earn me money. Ones that can help make me more of an asset to this world than a liability. I think if we all adopted the mindset of consuming more information than entertainment, success would become a lot easier to obtain.

BORN THROUGH A BOOK

I love the television show Shark Tank. I'll explain it for those who may not be familiar with it. Shark Tank gives entrepreneurs an opportunity to pitch venture capitalists for money to start or grow their businesses. I'm reminded of an episode where an entrepreneur named Michael Elliott was pitching his existing business called

Hammer and Nails. The business was designed to provide manicures and pedicures exclusively for men. At the end of his pitch, the sharks asked Elliot about his background. He explained to them that at 16 years old he was a ward of the state in Pennsylvania that spent his junior year of high school living in a youth shelter. By 18 he was living on the streets, and after two years of homelessness decided he wanted to make something of himself.

At this point, Elliot decided to save some money and publish the first ever Hip-Hop magazine on March 15, 1988 called Krush. The next year he saved $250 and produced a local Hip-Hop video show called Krush Rap, which he self-syndicated to 20 markets. He also became the Director of Special Projects for a well-known Hip-Hop magazine called The Source. After becoming burned out on Hip-Hop, he decided to move to California and write movies.

Elliot explained that he went to a book store and bought a book on screenwriting. Thirteen months later he sold his very first movie script to 20th Century Fox, which was eventually made into the movie "Brown Sugar" starring Taye Diggs and Sanaa Lathan. He explained that he also had a film in theaters called "Just Wright" starring Queen Latifah and the rapper Common. At the time of his appearance on Shark Tank, Elliot's movies had generated $118,000,000 at the box office.

Grow Into Success

Michael Elliot's screenwriting success was literally born through a book. By reading material that provided instruction and perhaps examples of what he wanted to achieve, Elliot was able to turn his ideas into the tangible products of written movie scripts. You can do the same. If you are interested in a specific subject or field, you can buy a book or check one out at the library to educate yourself in that field.

Although Elliot did not receive funding for his business on the show, he did give a valuable a lesson by sharing his story. The lesson was that even if you are a ward of the state that was homeless for two years, if you pick up a book and read about what interests you, you could very well do some amazing things that you never thought were possible for you.

Lyndell Johnson

EDUCATION RECAP

1. Recognize that education is more than just school work.

2. Read as much as you can about your chosen field.

3. Know that your success can be born through a book.

4. **EVOLVE THROUGH EDUCATION.**

Chapter 9
BECOME A MASTER OF TIME

"Time is the most precious element of human existence"
-DENIS WAITLEY

Each day we live brings us a day closer to death. We are blessed with a finite amount of time, and that time is inexplicably valuable. But many of us treat time as though it will never run out. We spend our time doing mindless things that only serve our cravings for entertainment, while the things that serve our purpose are put on the back burner.

There is a popular saying that time is money. I whole-heartedly disagree with this belief. Time is not money. The two couldn't be more different. As a matter of fact, time is a much more valuable resource than money could ever be. When you lose money, you can always gain more of it, but when you lose time it's gone forever. You can never get that time back, so you must use this precious commodity wisely and be as productive as possible with the time you do have.

Another popular myth is that there's not enough time in a day. Let's think about this. We each have 24 hours per day, 168 hours per week, 8,760 hours per year, yet some of us manage to get extraordinary things done during this time while others don't. Why is this? What is the one crucial factor that makes a person a master of his/her time instead of a slave to procrastination? PRIORITIES!!!

Prioritization is the magic bullet that can easily stop procrastination dead in its tracks. We all know we should prioritize our activities throughout the day, but some of us just fail to do so. Some of us have bought into the lie that there's just not enough time in a day. I believe we all have plenty of time to do the things we keep putting off for later. If we count eight hours per night for sleep, and eight hours per day for work, if we have a job, that still leaves eight hours left over per day. I know some people work more hours, sleep more or less hours, or have varying responsibilities that don't fit neatly into the 8/8/8 theory. My point is that no matter how your time is divided, prioritization is VITAL to your success. The key is to set aside time for the things that mean the most to us. What activities are high up on your list of priorities? Whether it's playing with your kids, cleaning around the house, or working on the book that you have been planning to write for the past 3 years, carve out at least 30 minutes to an hour to work on it daily. You might be surprised how much time you actually have to do those things you choose to prioritize.

FIX YOUR TIME WITH FOCUS

Have you ever heard someone say that they lost track of time? I know I have. This is a problem that many of us face, but it can be solved through the skill of focus. Time deprivation is caused by broken focus. In my everyday life, I realize that when my eye is on the clock, I get things done within the prescribed time. But when my mind wanders, and my focus is scattered, time seems to easily slip through my fingers.

My wife is also an author with a very busy schedule throughout the week. On top of writing books, she juggles school and recreational activities with our kids, online business marketing, coaching clients, and being a fantastic wife. How does she manage to get it all done without losing her mind? She simply focuses on what is important to her, and she starts early. Starting early is such a critical component of time management for several reasons. Here are just a few of them.

- ❖ It creates the illusion of having more hours in your day.
- ❖ You are full of fresh energy in the morning, which provides optimal motivation for tackling big tasks.

❖ You get to work in peace while most other people are asleep.

❖ You get more time to do the things you want to do by doing the things you have to do early.

❖ You just feel better when you are up early making meaningful use of your time, rather than waking up at the last minute and scrambling to get things done.

While getting started early is important, here is an even more important reason to master your time in my opinion. When I become old and gray, and my life is almost over, hopefully with family and friends surrounding my death bed, I want to look back over my life and feel that I lived. I want to feel that I made an impact on this world, and that I helped make it a better place because I was here. Because I decided to focus my time and energy around becoming a person that affected positive change in the lives of my fellow human beings. I don't want to die with a bunch of bottled up potential inside me that was never released. The only way to make sure that never happens is to get busy doing what I was born to do. What will you focus your time toward accomplishing? Will you allow focus to be the fix for your time management problems?

TIME BETWEEN TWO BROTHERS

Mark was a high school athlete with dreams of playing football in college and eventually turning pro. His parents had always taught him to use his time wisely if he wanted to be successful in life. Mark took their advice to heart, and spent his spare time doing things that were aligned with his goals. He woke up early and ran one hour, five days a week. Mark also spent time preparing healthy foods for himself in order to help maintain his athletic build. In addition to practice with his team after school, Mark also practiced drills with friends in his neighborhood after practice.

During weekends, rather than watching entertaining shows on television, Mark dedicated time to watching video recordings of past football games to discover where he made mistakes, and planned strategies to improve his performance for the next game. Mark seemed to have his priorities in order. He knew where he wanted to go, and was taking the necessary steps to get there. He even learned to enjoy spending time preparing for his future, because he understood that if he didn't enjoy the journey he would eventually give up on striving toward his goals. All the while, Mark kept his vision of college and NFL success at the forefront of his mind, eagerly awaiting his chance to advance.

In Mark's senior year of high school, he was scouted and recruited to play for one of his dream colleges. His coaches had been putting in a good word for him with several college coaches, because they knew he was a skillful player with an exceptional work ethic. He was also a respectable young man full of discipline and leadership abilities.

Because he had put in work for many years, Mark was now in position to step his game up to the next level. As he reflected on how he had arrived at his current station in life, Mark attributed his success to careful time management. He was one of the few players on his team to be recruited because he did what many other players would not do. He dedicated his spare time to developing himself into a better player, rather than hanging out with friends. He became smarter, faster, and stronger by immersing himself in activities that built him up. Mark continued to use time management strategies throughout his college football career. Although he was never drafted into the NFL, he was still a success in his own right. He proved to himself that great time management skills are key to success.

Mark's parents taught his younger brother, Tyler, the same lessons about time management that they taught him, but Tyler chose to use his time differently. He dreamed of attending Harvard Law school, but he was a couch potato. He spent his spare time playing video games and binge-watching Game of Thrones on television. Tyler knew that he should probably spend more time studying to get good grades for Harvard's acceptance, but he thought he was already smart enough to get the grades he needed.

Tyler's parents talked to him regularly about using his time more constructively, but their advice went in one ear and out the other. He figured he knew better than anyone what was best for him, even his parents. Mark also tried talking to his brother, but Tyler resented Mark. He felt Mark was the golden boy of the family, and only saw him as a nagging brother rather than a source of wisdom. Due to lack of study and preparation for school, Tyler's grades declined steadily throughout his senior year. Ultimately, his core class final grades were all Cs and Ds.

When time came to apply for Harvard Law School, Tyler was behind the curve. He submitted his application hoping to slip through the cracks and gain admission, but had no such luck. His Harvard dreams were crushed. In the end, Tyler blamed his parents for not pushing him harder when it was all his own fault.

This story is a great example of why time management is such an important skill. When we properly manage our time, we can achieve lifelong dreams. But when we mismanage that time we often suffer lifelong regrets. Dedicate your time to perfecting your craft and engaging in developmental activities that help prepare you for what is to come. The more you repeat these activities, the more of an expert you will become.

How well do you manage your time? Do you dedicate time to activities that help move you closer to fulfilling your goals and dreams, or do you spend hour after hour engaging in entertainment that has no benefit for your future? If the latter is your answer, it's never too late to change for the better. Set time aside to plan your priorities. For instance, if your goal is to save $300 this month, take time to figure out some things you can trim from your budget, if necessary. If you are unhappy with your job because they don't pay you enough money, and you can't get along with your boss, take time to update your resume and send it to potential employers rather than wasting time complaining about how much you hate it. Or better yet, start your own business and be your own boss. Taking time to work on solutions to your problems is an absolute must. Mastering your time can be a key component for mastering your life.

<u>TIME MASTERY RECAP</u>

1. Fix your time with focus.

2. Prioritize your goals and activities.

3. Don't waste your valuable time.

4. **BECOME A MASTER OF TIME.**

Chapter 10
PRACTICE THE ART OF PATIENCE

"Patience, persistence and perspiration make an unbeatable combination for success"
-NAPOLEON HILL

We live in a world where most people expect to achieve massive success overnight, but Rome wasn't built in a day, and neither is a life of success. Pinnacles can only be reached through a slow and gradual process consisting of small habits performed consistently over an extended period of time. If you are unwilling to develop patience and embrace the concept of slow and steady progress, you may never be successful.

Many of us had more patience as toddlers than we do as adults. We had the drive to achieve our goal of learning to walk in our early years, but lack the drive to achieve our goal of building success in our later years. If we would dare to muster up the internal fortitude to push ourselves, even in the midst of repeated failure, just as we learned to walk as children, we could learn to fly as adults. We could learn to live the visions we see in our minds, and barrel our way through any limits that we previously set for ourselves. The key is having the patience to wait.

THE MARATHON MENTALITY

Patience is the result of building your endurance. Marathon runners know this all too well. They understand they need to train themselves to tolerate long-distance running, so they cultivate the habit of running several miles daily, or every other day until they can complete the 26-mile trek. The journey to success is just like a marathon, not a sprint. If you attempt to sprint your way to greatness by expecting grand results too soon, you will likely burn out pretty fast. You will quit in your mind, because the finish line you seek is beyond your sight.

When you choose to adopt the marathon mindset, your expectation of fast results changes. When your expectation changes, so does the way you approach success. You begin to adjust your habits to fit your new mindset, and the frustration that stems from impatience begins to go away. Here are just a few of the habits that can help you shape the marathon mentality.

Lyndell Johnson

1. Delaying Gratification

Learning to delay gratification is such a powerful tool. Forming this habit could enable you to lose weight in a healthy way, save/make more money, and be more appreciative of your success. For example, if you were to diet and lose one pound a week for one year, you would lose 52 pounds throughout that year. That's much better than no pounds, even though it takes a year.

If you were to invest your money, instead of spending it on something you want right now, you could gain more money by being patient enough to let your money sit in an investment account. Instant gratification such as credit card purchases could cause you to lose money if you don't have the money to pay on time later. There is no fun in paying late fees and higher interest charges. In fact, these extra fees and higher charges can ruin you financially simply because you failed to delay gratification.

Delaying gratification also allows you to cherish the fruits of your labor more. We value and appreciate our rewards more when we have to work for and wait on them. That's why so many lottery winners go broke in a few years. When the reward comes easily, it often goes easily. If you have been saving millions over many years, you are much less likely to blow it in a short period of time, because of the pain associated with its accumulation. Ripened fruit is much sweeter than unripe, but you must be willing to wait fir it.

2. Nipping Anxiety in the Bud

Anxiety is a huge barrier when attempting to adopt the marathon mentality. Worrying about whether or not you will ever reach your goal creates doubt in your mind. When you doubt, it hinders your ability to take action and draws you further away from your goals.

To avoid anxiety during their long journey, many marathon runners use the joyful distraction of music. Adding an activity that helps keep your mind off the time it takes to achieve your goals can help cure your anxiety problems. Next time you feel your dream is taking too long, and you start to get anxious, indulge in a fun activity that gives you renewed energy.

Taking a break when you feel mentally fatigued can be a lifesaver. Exercise is a great stress reliever for the brain and body. Get out for a nice walk or run to release nervous energy and bring yourself back down to earth. A journey that is uneventful is usually a boring journey. That's why most people make musical playlists for road trips. Strive to keep your mind and body occupied, instead of counting the minutes until you reach your goals. After all, the grass doesn't grow faster when you sit and watch.

3. Staying Fueled Up

When marathon runners hit the road, they ensure they have the proper nutrition to sustain themselves throughout the journey.

They make sure they get sufficient amounts of carbohydrates, protein, and water or Gatorade to prevent ending up sidelined in the middle of their run.

The same approach should be implemented on your journey to success. Just as the runner needs healthy fuels for the body, you will need healthy fuels for your mind in the form of literature that promotes mental growth. As the journey to success becomes harder to navigate due to unavoidable adversities and circumstances, you will need knowledge of how others that came before you made it through similar situations. This information can be found in the biographies of those that are currently in the position you are striving to reach. Stay open to variety, because it is the spice of life. New information can bring something alive in you that you once believed to be dead. So, when the going gets tough those that are tough get food for thought that helps them cross the finish line of success.

MEDICINE FOR MEDIOCRITY

I remember a time when I was my own worst enemy. Every time I thought of writing books or working towards other goals, I was stopped in my tracks by thoughts of how long it would take to achieve them. I quickly realized that impatience was a mental condition that held me back from the life I wanted, but one day the cure came to me in the form of an "aha" moment.

I thought about the difference between buying fast food and preparing home cooked meals. Many of us are drawn to McDonald's, Burger King, and other fast food restaurants because the food is prepared quickly, most times. Especially after work, when we are hungry and in a rush to get home and feed ourselves and our families. We are eager to flock to the drive-thru for a quick fix, but here's the problem. Most fast food is bad for you. Nutrition is largely sacrificed for speed.

On the flip side, when we prepare meals at home, we have more control of what we put in our bodies. Also, preparing your own meals is often cheaper than take out. Although it might take longer to cook your own food, it is often the better choice for your health as well as your wallet. In this scenario, the cure for poor/mediocre health and finances is avoiding the quick fix, and having enough patience to buy and cook food for yourself.

Likewise, in your business or career endeavors, you should focus on taking time to create your success. You must find and collect the necessary ingredients to cook up a fulfilling business or career. The ingredients are the habits you form that support your vision. Let patience be one of those main ingredients. Don't let impatience force you into mediocrity. You know deep down inside that you are filled with something this world needs. Will you allow it to die inside of you by giving up on yourself, or will you patiently grow into your life's work? Understand that although your goals and dreams may take time to manifest, they will surely come to pass. Have faith that it is on the way, and hold on to the picture of victory in your mind. A patient heart will give you the inner strength to go beyond the boundaries you once thought held you back. If you can master the art of patience, nothing will be able to stop you from conquering the world except you!

PATIENCE RECAP

1. Adopt the marathon mentality.

2. Take the cure for mediocrity.

3. Take your time and grow into success.

4. **PRACTICE THE ART OF PATIENCE.**

CONCLUSION

There you have it. Ten of the most important keys for growing into success. They will work for you if you do the work. If you put forth the necessary sweat equity, doors will open in your life like you never dreamed of. But it will take commitment, discovery of purpose, bravery, avoiding negative chatter, taking action, building your willpower, seeing yourself as the rock star that you are, evolution through education, mastering your time, and the patience to wait through the growing process.

You have what it takes to be a millionaire, a world changer, the best in your field, an inspiration to others, a servant to those in need, a giver of valuable knowledge and skill, and a superhero among mere mortals. But first you must take what you learn and put it into practice. Take the knowledge and growth you acquire and apply it on a daily basis. This will put you on the path to glory, which will not only enable you to grow the things you have, but to grow who you are as a person. It will help you increase your self-worth, because the substance and essence who of you are will be magnified. Can you see yourself being a better you? Can you see yourself executing the things in life you always wanted to do? Now is the time to seize your destiny and grow into who you always knew you could be. THE MASTER OF YOUR OWN SUCCESS.

www.ingramcontent.com/pod-product-compliance
Lightning Source LLC
Chambersburg PA
CBHW051817040426
42446CB00007B/720